ANIMAL Elephant DIARIES

STEVE PARKER

QEB

Copyright © QEB Publishing 2014

First published in the United States in 2014 by
QEB Publishing, Inc.
3 Wrigley, Suite A
Irvine, CA 92618
www.qed-publishing.co.uk

A CIP record for this book is available from the Library of Congress.

ISBN 978 1 60992 613 7

Editor Carey Scott
Illustrator Peter David Scott/The Art Agency
Designer Dave Ball
Editorial Assistant Tasha Percy
Managing Editor Victoria Garrard

Printed and bound in China

Photo Credits
Key: t = top, b = bottom, l = left, r = right, c = center,
FC = front cover, BC = back cover.
Alamy Gabriela Staebler/Corbis Cusp 27 br, World Photo 19 tr; **Corbis** Roger
de la Harpe 28 bl, George Steinmetz 24 cl, Paul Souders 7 tr, Christian Kober/
Robert Harding World Imagery 21 br; **FLPA** Conrad Wathe/Minden Pictures
27 br; **Getty Images** Oxford Scientific 23 br, Franco Barfi/Waterframe 27 br;
Shutterstock HomeStudio 11 br, EcoPrint 10 tl, Noel Powell 11 bc, Kristina
Postnikova, Gordan, David M. Schrader, Luminis, Oleg Glovnev, Ana de Sousa,
Valentin Agapov, Dementeva, Petr Jilek all background images

Contents

check out my trunk!

Forest of Legs

My first memory is lots and lots of big, tall legs all around me. It was sunrise and I was lying on the ground, just born. My Mom was closest. Then, one by one, the other mothers in My Herd all came for a look. They sniffed and stroked me with their trunks. It was wonderful!

Me trotting next to My Mom.

African Savanna Elephant

Adult size

Length 20 feet

Height 13 feet

Weight 13,000 pounds

Habitat Bush, grassland, open woods

Food Leaves, grass, twigs, fruits, shoots, flowers, bark

Features Massive! Huge ears, long nose trunk, big tusks

Next I remember standing up—and falling down. After a few hours of practice I could walk. I stayed touching My Mom, trying not to get under her big feet.

My Herd relaxed in the hot sun while I practiced walking, and then running. In the evening, My Herd began to search for food. I had to trot fast to keep up with them!

My Mom says the stripy ones are seebraz zebras.

My birth was big news!

My Mom's feet are massive, but she's very careful where she steps.

Baby elephants can hardly see at first, so we use our trunk to feel and smell. It took me a while to learn how to move mine—I tripped over it a couple of times.

NEW CALF FOR SUNRISE HERD

The new calf with Mother and Aunt.

Just before dawn this morning, a mother elephant in the Sunrise Herd gave birth to a healthy calf, weighing 234 pounds. The birth took slightly less than two hours, and the baby could stand after another two. A spokes-elephant said: "We are all thrilled at the addition to our group, which takes our number to 37. Mother and baby are both doing well."

My Herd

I'm getting to know the elephants in My Herd. The grown-ups are all females, or cows. The oldest is Wise One. She's the boss and leads us from place to place. Then there's My Sister and lots of Aunts and Cousins.

Some grown-ups can doze standing up. Respect!

All of the herd sniff, look, and listen for danger.

Big Aunt is munching some leafy twigs.

My Mom says that our herd is called the Sunrise Herd. As the sun comes up at dawn, we stand sideways to warm up quickly as we feed. By midday it's so hot we doze in the shade. As the sun begins to set, we become active again, and it's playtime for us young ones.

Wise One is so old that she even falls asleep during the day.

I remember the first time I met Snout the Rhino. He was standing next to a bush, looking and sniffing. He's almost as big as us elephants. He also has a long nose but it's stiff and sharp, not bendy and useful like our trunk.

Best Aunt watches the youngsters playing.

Snout's thick skin is almost as stiff as tree bark.

Sister is playfighting with Second Cousin.

First Cousin is almost a grown-up.

I'm now starting to move farther away from My Mom. Not too far though—never more than a couple of feet. Every hour or two I go back to feed on her milk, and she strokes me with her trunk. So nice! If the other elephants make a warning sound, like a snort or a stamp, I rush back and hide behind her legs.

I love My Mom. Sometimes she scolds me, but she also feeds me and protects me.

7

Learning Is Fun!

Every day I learn new things. It's difficult to control a trunk, two big ears, four legs, and a tail too. But once I learn, I don't forget. Elephants have fantastic. . . er, what's the word. . . memories.

Yesterday I learned to flap my ears when I felt too hot. My ~~blud~~ blood carries the warmth from my body into my huge ears, which fan the air to lose the heat. Cool!

I breathe through holes called nostrils.

My trunk is my joined-up nose and upper lip, stretched out very long.

My ears flap in the breeze.

Milk comes from the teats on My Mom's front belly.

I'll be drinking My Mom's milk for about five years. She stands quietly while I drink lots and get completely full. Of course, an hour later I'm hungry again!

Sometimes My Mom and I stand and rest together. She dangles her trunk next to me, sniffs gently, and touches me. I sniff her too. We know each other as much by smell as by sight. My Mom's wonderful!

My skin is thick but bendy.

I can sleep safe with My Mom.

Six-month-old Fourth Cousin has started eating plants now.

My tail is tricky to control. The grown-ups use their tails to swish away pesky flies and bugs.

THINGS TO PRACTICE WITH MY TRUNK

1. Stroke My Mom

2. Sniff the air

3. Blow dust

4. Pull down leaves and twigs

5. Pull up grass

6. Suck up water to squirt into my mouth and drink. Or to spray over me—cool!

On the Move

Wise One said it's time to move on because we've eaten most of the food around here. She sniffed the air, listened hard, and set off past The Big Hills. So now we're looking for a place where it has rained recently, where there will be new grass and fresh leaves on the trees.

I ate the last acacia seed pod. Yum!

My Mom walks beside me.

WHAT I ATE TODAY

1. My Mom's milk (but there's less every day)
2. Baobab buds
3. Acacia seed pods
4. Bermuda grass

As we walked, some Long-Necks joined us. We like them to travel with us because they make really tall lookouts. Also, the killer animals we call Sharp-Tooths are less likely to attack a really big group, because we can all charge at them.

Wise One is now 60 years old, and she's been leading the Sunrise Herd for 20 years. She remembers all the places we've been, and knows which ones have food at each time of year, and which areas have dangerous Sharp-Tooths.

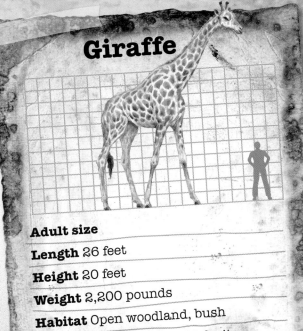

Giraffe

Adult size

Length 26 feet

Height 20 feet

Weight 2,200 pounds

Habitat Open woodland, bush

Food Leaves, twigs, buds, fruits, shrubs, grasses

Features Very long neck and legs, small horns

Long-Necks are the tallest animals.

We follow where Wise One steps.

Wise One always leads the herd.

Dry bark. Yuk!

Hard, sharp, dead grass. Ugh!

Danger!

Whoaaa, NOW I am afraid of Sharp-Tooths! My Mom, a few Aunts (I can't remember which ones), and I have been surrounded by Sandy Ones. They scarily crept up when we got separated from the main herd.

Big Aunt waves her ears to look even bigger.

Spotty Snarlers wait to see what happens.

This Sandy One is challenging Aunt.

I stay between My Mom and Aunts.

Spotted Hyena

Adult size

Length Around 5 feet

Height Up to 3 feet

Weight 130 pounds

Habitat Open woodland, bush, grassland

Food Any animals, from rats to elephants, alive or dead

Features Sharp senses, strong crunching teeth, can run for hours, group hunting

On the flat ~~savaaanh~~ grasslands, I'm learning about how ~~kwikly~~ quickly killers can appear from nowhere. (I'm so scared, I can't spell.) Not only Sandies, but also Spotty Snarlers. They usually hang back, wait for the Sandies to make the kill, then come in and crunch up the remains.

My Mom makes a loud trumpet noise to frighten the Sharp-Tooths.

Sandies look like clumps of grass until they move. I've learned to see and smell their pawprints to work out if the danger is still near. Luckily, this time My Mom and the Aunts scared them all away. Result!

A Sandy One's pawprint.

This Sandy One's around the back!

The chief Sandy One is ready to attack from the front.

Lioness

Adult size (female, they do all the hunting)

Length 8 feet

Height 3 feet

Weight 330 pounds

Habitat Grassland, open woodland, bush

Food Wildebeest, zebra, antelopes—and young elephants!

Features Long sharp teeth, powerful body, keen senses, group hunting

Trek to Salt Cave

It's my first trip to Salt Cave. My Mom says that Sunrise Herd go there a couple of times every year. It's a huge hole in the cliff where we can eat tons of salty-tasting soil from the floor and walls. It's a long journey there, but of course Wise One knows the way.

Acacia trees have become dry and hard.

The Thorn Clump is dry, dusty, and dull.

Wise One led as we started the journey.

Other animals say that elephants are clumsy, but actually we are really good at walking quietly and neatly. Our wide feet spread out our body weight along narrow paths. We can easily tiptoe up steep slopes, over sand, and across mud.

The Waterhole is too small for a fun bath.

My Herd hurries me along to Salt Cave. Its soil gives us stuff called minerals, which we need to stay healthy. That's why we eat other strange things too—even poop! It's to get nutrients that are missing from our main foods.

WEIRD THINGS I EAT

1. Horrible-tasting salty soil

2. Awful-tasting salty mud

3. Bugs and worms, for vitamins

4. Droppings from My Mom

5. Pee from others in My Herd

Being small, I was safe along The Cliff.

Being small, I was in danger at The Falls. My Mom helped me.

We loosen the soil with our tusks.

It's a steep path down to Salt Cave.

Now I'm at Salt Cave, there's a problem. The soil tastes disgusting! My Mom tells me to eat up, otherwise I won't be allowed any nice foods afterward, like acacia seed pods. So unfair!

15

Strange Creatures

Today was soooo strange. I saw some new animals out on the plains. They walk on two legs—weird. They go fast in a big noisy Shell—odd. They don't eat leaves—creepy. They make loud noises, and their Shell is even louder—awful!

I moved my ears to hear as much as possible.

Human

Adult size

Height 5-6 feet

Weight 110-220 pounds

Habitat Anywhere

Food Anything

Features Walks on two legs. Very clever

Wise One says that these creatures are called Humans. They always bring trouble. Last time they came, there were some really loud banging noises, a bit like sharp thunder. Then, some of Sunrise Herd disappeared forever.

The Human Shell is really peculiar. We've never seen it eat, but it drinks about once each day. It can run for hours without tiring. However, it has trouble with rocky places and deep mud. I'll remember that, because I don't trust it.

The Human Shell is still and silent for ages, not like a real animal.

We watched the Humans and their Shell for almost half the day. Then at dusk, they left the area. But My Mom, Fourth Cousin, and Little Aunt say the Humans will be back. Something bad happened last time they came, and it might happen again.

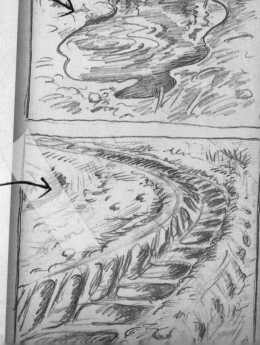

I hear the Shell's noise, like a Sharp-Tooth's growl but much longer.

The Humans sometimes have small eyes, then they go really big.

I taste the horrid oily liquid the Shell leaves in the soil. Ugh!

The Shell leaves long pawprints behind.

Saddest Day

My Herd is so unhappy. Humans came early this morning. There were bangs, and now Best Aunt is dead. She was my favorite, and still young at 27. She didn't starve or get an illness, she just fell and died. No time to say good-bye. How unnatural is that!

My Mom tried to lift the body and bring it back to life.

Wise One put some leaves and twigs on the body.

When one of My Herd dies, we stand around the body, touching it with our trunks and feet. It's said there are special places called elephant graveyards, where old ones go to die. But this ancient tale isn't true.

My Mom says next time we come this way there'll be only bones left. Spotty Snarlers tear the skin, and Hook-Beaks called vultures peck the flesh away.

Scavengers soon gather around a carcass.

The oddest thing is that Best Aunt has lost her tusks. They are nowhere to be seen. I think the Humans took them. Why they need tusks, I can't imagine—their mouths are much too small. I'll remember this awful day for the rest of my life.

Little Aunt made lots of rumbling noises.

TUSKS ARE USEFUL FOR . . .

1. Pushing over trees to eat

2. Digging up roots for food

3. Ripping off soft bark to chew

4. Fighting off Sharp-Tooths

5. Fighting battles at mating time

Dry Season

There's been no rain for weeks. The leaves and grass are brown. I've been talking to other Green-Eaters about what they like to bite and chew. It seems we all like different things, so we won't have to fight over food.

Every zebra has slightly different stripes.

Swift uses his hard hooves to kick at enemies.

Stripey the zebra often grazes near us. She can eat the toughest, stringy, thick grasses, which other Green-Eaters avoid. She also munches on low-growing plants.

Swift the Thomson's gazelle also likes grasses, and he can survive on really dry, crisp ones that would make me choke. Swift also noses in the soil for seeds and bits of old plants. He's really nice!

THINGS TO DO . . .
1. Look for food
2. Have a dust bath—there's plenty of dust!
3. Look for food some more
4. Play with Sister
5. Look for food again

Grunt the wildebeest has a blunt nose and wide, sharp front teeth. She can get right down to the ground and bite off broad mouthfuls of really short grasses. Even my amazing trunk could not do that!

Grunt defends herself with her sharp horns.

Spring leaps over bushes to escape Sharp-Tooths.

Spring the kudu can rear up on his back legs to reach high food. Like me, he eats mainly leaves, buds, shoots, and fruits. But Spring also likes flowers and trailing vines, which I usually leave.

The Big Waterhole is now so small, it gets crowded with Green-Eaters.

Fire!

PANIC! A lightning flash hit a bush and it caught alight. The birds squawked an alert before flying away to safety. If only we could fly too! The dry grass and trees crackle and burn, and the flames race even faster than we can run.

The smell, noise, and heat are terrifying!

The flames are burning this tree, but it should recover.

RUN! This is my first fire, and I'm going to stay right next to My Mom! She is looking for a gap in the blaze where we can escape, or perhaps some rocks or a pool where the fire can't follow us.

At last all the Sunrise Herd is safe. It's lucky the birds called their warnings. Wise One says they are "feathered fire alarms." Now they gather around the edges of the burned area, ready to eat the creatures fleeing the heat.

Cattle egrets squabble over a place on our back.

Egret searching the ground for bugs, mice, frogs, and lizards.

The birds are helpful in other ways too. They perch on us and peck off pests to eat, such as flies, ticks, and other bugs. We get our skin cleaned, and they get a tasty snack. Neat!

As we hurry on, we come to an area that has had a recent fire. The thunderstorm put out the flames and watered the soil. The plants are already growing through the damp earth. Isn't nature amazing?

Seeds in the soil survive and soon start to grow.

23

Rains at Last

Wise One's old but she still loves a mudbath!

Wise One was first to sniff the air, see the distant dark clouds, and hear the thunder. She knew that the rains were coming. It happens at about the same time each year. The raindrops splashed on my body, cooled me down, and made puddles to drink from. After all the dust and dryness, rain is great!

DROUGHT OVER: MIGRATION BEGINS

Heavy traffic on Migration Route 2B

The dry season ended yesterday as storms and rain swept across the Great Plain. "Thank goodness" said a spokes-zebra. "We were beginning to think the rains would never come." Wildebeest and antelopes lined up along main Migration Routes 1C and 2B. Nine gazelles were swept away or caught by crocodiles as they crossed the now-rushing Big River.

Sister is about to dive under and breathe through her lifted-up trunk.

Soon the waterholes filled up. Elephants love to squish, squelch, roll, and ~~wolwal~~ wallow in mud. It gets bugs and pests off our skin, helps wounds to heal, and keeps us cool. I've learned to suck water up my trunk and blow it out to give myself a shower.

Nile Crocodile

Adult size

Length 16.5 feet

Height 2.6 feet

Weight 1,100 pounds

Habitat Rivers, lakes, swamps, marshes

Food Many animals including zebras, antelopes—even elephants!

Features Strong jaws, pointed teeth, powerful tail, lurks underwater

Hippo is sleepy by day.

I was just having a fun shower when . . .

. . . Croc floated to the surface. Arrggh, run!

Hippo spends all day in the water, then comes on land at night to eat plants. Croc likes it too —but that's the problem. She's one of the most dangerous Sharp-Tooths. She may suddenly swish her tail to lunge forward and bite hard. She especially likes to catch youngsters like me.

Little Aunt is the best mud-roller.

25

Big Visitors

Elephants use sounds a lot to "talk." We make rumbles and purrs so low, Humans can't hear them. We also bellow, trumpet, squeak, and snort, usually when we're worried or afraid. But today I heard the loudest noises ever, made by elephants I'd never seen before.

Two bulls roar, push and shove.

My Mom says the big visitors are bulls—grown-up males. They arrive once each year, to show off, bellow loudly, and fight each other furiously. The winners mate with the grown-up females, known as cows.

My Mom says that one of the biggest bulls is My Dad. Soon all the bulls will be gone. When they are young grown-ups, they sometimes live together in loose groups. As they get older, they mostly live alone.

Bulls have bigger tusks than cows.

As My Dad fights a rival, the ground shakes!

When a bull and a cow get together they move away from the main herd. They sniff each other, flap ears, rub heads, click tusks, and stroke each other with their trunks.

Moms are usually the leaders.

A New Wise One

Two days ago, Wise One got sooo tired. She lay down and went to sleep and we just couldn't wake her. It was like when Best Aunt died—but slower. We had time to say good-bye. Very sad. Now we need a new leader.

Me, My Mom, and some others got ~~sepreated~~ separated from the main herd. We tried to find our usual route, but fences and Human Shells were in the way.

Shells up ahead! New Wise One must decide where to go next.

Wherever we turn, the Shells wait and watch.

Young cousins trust our new Wise One to keep us safe!

These Human Shells are becoming sooo annoying! There seem to be many more of them now. They wake us when we're resting and get in our way when we're on the move.

THINGS TO REMEMBER . . .

1. Stay with the herd
2. Always look out for Sharp-Tooths
3. Don't forget important stuff

The Sunrise Herd decided that My Mom is the new Wise One. Awesome! She knows where to go to eat, drink, rest, and stay safe. But she's still My Mom, and she's still amazing! Maybe one day I could even be the Wise One.

I'll stay at the back to make sure everyone's okay.

What They Say About Me

My diary describes what I think of all the creatures I meet. But what do they think about me? Let's find out . . .

Zebra

> I love the first bite of a freshly killed elephant! But it's not a common meal for me. Us lionesses, who do the hunting, know that if you take on one elephant, you take on the whole herd.

Lioness

> Elephants are pests, simple as that. They eat too much, their bathing muddies the water, and they leave mountains of droppings everywhere. Plus they don't have stripes!

> I like the Sunrise Herd elephants. They use their strength, tusks, and trunks to push over trees and pull down branches. Then I can reach the extra food. Come on you ~~Hoodies~~ Herdies!

Giraffe

> We like traveling with the Sunrise Herd. We can see far from high up, and the elephants smell well from low down. It's a cool partnership.

Kudu

Crocodile

> A grown-up elephant is too big for me to grab and pull into the water. But a cute young elephant, with a tubby body, is much tastier—I mean, nicer (hee-hee).

Tricky Terms

Bulls Male animals of various kinds—cattle, whales, hippos, crocodiles—and elephants.

Cows Female animals of various kinds, including elephants.

Carcass The dead body of an animal.

Drought An exceptionally long dry time, when no rain falls, and plants and animals begin to suffer and die.

Dry season A long period with no rain. Dry seasons happen most years, so the local plants and animals are used to them.

Green-Eaters Plant-eating animals, also known as herbivores.

Hook-Beaks The Sunrise Herd's name for big birds with hook-shaped beaks or bills. They include eagles, who tend to hunt living prey, and vultures, who often feed on already dead bodies, or carcasses.

Human Shells What humans call cars and trucks—metal containers or shells around their driver and passengers.

Long-Necks The Sunrise Herd's name for giraffes, animals with very long necks and almost equally long front legs. Their total height can be almost 20 feet (6 m).

Migration A long journey to move between places that have the best conditions, such as food and shelter.

Nutrients Chemicals that bodies need to stay healthy. Vitamins and minerals are nutrients.

Salt Cave A cave, overhang, cliff, lake edge, or similar place where the soil is rich in minerals such as salt. Like most wild creatures, elephants know when they need these minerals. Their normal food lacks them, so the elephants search them out.

Sandies The Sunrise Herd's name for lions, whose sandy-colored or tawny fur blends in with the dry grasses to give them excellent camouflage.

Scavengers Animals that feed mainly on already-dead and perhaps rotting bodies or carcasses, rather than hunting and killing live victims or prey and eating fresh meat.

Sharp-Tooths The Sunrise Herd's name for various predators or meat-eating animals, also known as carnivores. They include big cats such as lions, leopards, and cheetahs, and also hyenas.

Spotty Snarlers The Sunrise Herd's name for the predatory or meat-eating animals called hyenas, which in this part of Africa have spotted coats.

Waterhole In a generally dry area, a pond, pool, or lake that has water for most of the year. Animals go there to drink.

> We're known as cowardly scavengers, but that's so unfair. When we're really hungry, we can attack as a group and even kill a grown-up elephant. It's not easy, but it's a big feed!

Hyena

31

Index